Lethal Light

Lethal Light

Rozalli Lai

iUniverse, Inc.
New York   Bloomington

Lethal Light

Copyright ©2008 by Rozalli Lai

iUniverse books may be ordered through booksellers or by contacting:

iUniverse
1663 Liberty Drive
Bloomington, IN 47403
www.iuniverse.com
1-800-Authors (1-800-288-4677)

ISBN: 978-0-595-50975-1 (pbk)
ISBN: 978-0-595-61717-3 (ebk)

Printed in the United States of America

iUniverse rev. date: 11/07/08

Dedication

*For inspiration to everyone who is fighting anorexia, and
Dr. P. Jaffer, Dr. C. L. Birmingham, Dr. B. Griffin,
Rob McLeod, St. Paul's Hospital, Orenda House & Pathways from EFRY
Society and all my friends.*

I love you. I will continue to pray for all.

Acknowledgement

The writing of this book would not have been possible without the continuous and genuine support and encouragements from my care team: Dr. P. Jaffer, Dr. C. L. Birmingham and all staff from the St. Paul's Hospital Eating Disorders Program, Elizabeth Fry Society, Orenda House, Pathways Program and Rob McLeod.

I would also like to thank everyone who supported me and walked me through this difficult journey of my life. Thank you from the bottom of my heart. Special thanks to: Paraluman, Nina, Julia, Ms. Smith, Ms. Cordoni, Mrs. Mushens, Femmie, Duncan, Jun, Peter, Mun Mun, Linda, my family and all the rest of my friends, especially Winnie, Beth, Tracy, Tama, and Angel.

All the blessings and guidance God has given me will never be forgotten. He picked me up from the many times I've fallen and wanted to give up. The Lord answers all my prayers, even unspoken ones. In the Lord, I found comfort and strength, for I am weak. I held on to life with the little strength I had left.

May endless blessings from God fill everyone's heart with happiness forever. Thank you.

~ *Foreword* ~

It all started when I was at the age of 17. In October 2005, I had my first episode of depression diagnosed. I was hospitalized in March 2006 for a suicide attempt. From then on, I was in and out of hospitals and ended up staying in 2 different hospitals for a total of 6 months.

What contributed to my depression? I think there were many triggers. It was my high school graduation year. I was trying to stay on top of my studies and run 2 school teams with all my other extracurricular activities, such as: piano and theory lessons, Chinese classes, volunteering in the hospital, a private care home and with St. John Ambulance. Stressing out and being a perfectionist was definitely one of the causes. I think my childhood traumas would have to be the second leading cause – the post traumatic stress disorder (PTSD) was always there and was released now in my early adulthood.

The anxiety of dealing with these situations led up to my "wanting to take control" over my life. I felt like everyone was controlling me, including medications. I was often told what I can and cannot do. It's my life! Don't I get to make any decisions?

It felt so good when I finally had a grasp of control in my hands, I didn't know how to let go, and therefore I took it way too far, which led to my obsessive control over food and body image. Not long after my first hospitalization, I had gone from 110 lbs. down to 75 lbs with my height of 5'1".

In this book, I will try to put in my thoughts and feelings experienced during my eating disorder. This book is a real life experience. Sometimes, there will be graphic descriptions of details during my fight with anorexia. Please stay and bear with me while I share my story with all of you.

I want to be a responsible writer and give fair warnings to my readers. Please do not attempt or engage in any of the behaviors and actions that may induce self-harm. The purpose of this book is to share my deepest feelings and inspire all to have a better understanding of anorexia. It is not intended as a weight-loss or self-mutilation guide.

Chapters are based on my weight at the time.

I hope you enjoy reading. Please feel free to recommend this book to inspire your loved ones.

Part One:
The Diagnosis (Dx)

95

I twirled around in front of the mirror twice, looking at the way my body looked. I modeled forward, backwards and sideways, pleased with the way I looked. I was pleased to have lost some weight without trying, though I was always a petite 5'1" girl. Depression gave me an excuse to skip meals because I'm not hungry. All I wanted to do was sleep all day, hide under my covers and cry. What more can a young girl do in a psychiatric unit when there's no one her age to talk to? The place is so boring.

The sun was shining and birds were chirping in a typical March morning. I went out on to the patio, which is the smoking pit for people who aren't allowed out like me. The smell of cigarettes stinks and makes me cough and gag. Nasty. I want out of this crap hole! I want to get out and breathe the fresh air without being surrounded by smoke. I feel like a caged animal, trapped with no where to go. Let me out! Where's the shrink?!

Doctors. They have all the control. It's 10 o'clock now. When's my psychiatrist coming to see me? Tick tock… tick tock, time became a liquid as every hour melted into another.

13:30. Finally, the shrink comes into my room and talks to me. We had a long talk of keeping me safe and I was going to be stuck here for a while just so I can be monitored.
As usual, I skipped breakfast and lunch. I was never a breakfast eater, but I usually eat lunch. I guess I just wasn't hungry.

I pretty much slept through the whole day. Nurses woke me up occasionally to check in on me and see how I'm feeling. Whatever, it's just another typical boring day in an adult psychiatric ward. It sucks to be an in-patient. At least I can stay cooped up and warm under my layers and layers of blankets.

When I am awake, I stare at the ceiling or walk around the ward. I don't know how or what I feel. Definitely, I feel anxious and depressed being stuck here. But honestly, what if they let me go? Am I going to attempt suicide again? Maybe in a more lethal way. In a way, I guess I feel safer than being out in the community, but I don't want to be dependant on the hospital to keep me alive. Many people are waiting for the bed I'm using. I feel guilty.

Why can't I control my urges to self harm and stay out of the hospital? What is wrong with me? I'm not happy with my life, obviously. I do want to take my life. This is so wrong! My life belongs to God. The Lord gave me the gift of life, so he should be the only one to take it away. O Lord, please hear me cry and guide me.

I'm such a selfish idiot who's too consumed in suicide plans that I lose consciousness to my surroundings. It is a sin. I can't focus myself on getting well.

I'm running out of hope. I'm exhausted from the recurrent nightmares and thoughts that consume me day and night. Why is it so dark inside?

Now, I'm just sitting here crying, helpless, not knowing what to do. I long for the traumatizing experiences and flashbacks to leave me alone. Please don't re-visit me again: *Don't touch me! Stop it! I don't want you to touch me! Please, don't make me... I'm your cousin! How could you? Why me? Nooooo...*

By the time the vivid memories in the flashbacks are finally over, I cry. Tears are streaming down my face. Nobody knows my secret. Not my parents. Not anyone.

The first time I made the disclosure was to my psychiatrist. He's sorry that it happened to me. I had nothing else to say and didn't really want to talk about it, so I redirected the topic to something else. I don't ever want to be reminded of it. All I want to do is forget. Maybe therapy helps. But I truly don't know. I don't have any strength left in me to face anything now.

I am weary of all my groaning; all the night make I my bed to swim; I water my couch with my tears.(Psalm 6.6) Teach me thy way, O Lord, and lead me in plain path, because of mine enemies. (Psalm 27.11)

I will continue to pray to You and ask You for help. Please lead the path to my paradise. For You are my Shepard, guide me, hold me, I long to follow You.

After seeing the psychiatrist, he asked the nursing staff to weigh me every week, because he was concerned about my weight. Apparently, it seems obvious that I have lost weight. 95 lbs. It was the magic number. I am happy with my weight. I feel great. I'm denying any weight problems or issues with eating, although everyone around me seemed to be quite concerned. But after all, I didn't TRY to lose weight. Did I? I just didn't eat because I didn't have an appetite. I also didn't want to sit around and gain weight.

92

How did I manage to lose 3 pounds in a week? I am NOT trying to restrict my food intake. Now, I have to drink that nasty meal replacement crap. Great.

At this stage of time, I'm still in denial of having an eating disorder. I didn't want to admit it. I didn't want help. I wanted to look good. The skinnier I am the better I would feel and look. Right? Food is not one of my interests right now. My stomach is growling at me, but that's what I have to do: starve myself in order to look the way I want to look. My stomach isn't flat enough. My arms look flabby and fat. My thighs are so disgusting and fat looking. I feel so ugly and just so overweight. Hmm… Maybe if I lost just a couple more pounds, I'd look better.

My self-perception is just distorted. But I didn't know it. I thought it was normal for every girl to want to lose weight and diet. I always envied girls that were skinnier than I was. I compare myself to all other girls in my sight. She's fat. She's skinny. She has a perfect body. I start to criticize my own body and try to make my body look the way I want it to look. I have control over this. I can't control my emotions, but I certainly can control my eating habits and make myself look better.

This is all about control. I've had many suicide attempts. If I were to seriously count them up, I would say at least 15 times in this year with just mainly overdosing and sometimes cutting. Some drug overdoses were lethal enough that I ended up in CCU for days with tubes and wires stuck to every part of my body. I couldn't move. I had to pee in a catheter, in a bag. I kept on throwing up charcoal. I couldn't stop throwing up. I'm losing it. I'm losing all my control. I can't control what they do to me anymore. I'm certified under the Mental Health Act. I'm incapable of making my own decisions regarding my safety. Medications control me. They mess with my brain for some kind of chemical imbalance. Since I can't control anything in my life, I think the only control I have left is to control what I eat.

Nobody can make me eat if I didn't want to. I feel like I'm being controlled. I don't like the feeling of that. I want to be able to do things my own way; therefore, I took every chance there was to grasp tight control over anything or anyone I had. I feel hostile and angry at myself and everyone.

It feels so good to have a magic wand at hand. I can make anything happen. Control. I've been longing for that. I'm going to eat less. I started to look at all the caloric content of every single thing I put in my mouth. I wouldn't let myself have more than 1000 calories per day. Sometimes, if I did go over my mental limit of 1000 calories, I'd feel so guilty and restricted more the next day to make up for it the next day.

I got weighed again. Needless to ask, of course I wanted to know how much I weighed! 91 pounds. Another pound to worry about. I'm still not satisfied with the way I looked in the mirror. I feel so alone. Sometimes, I feel like the reflection of the girl I see in the mirror is my only true friend. No one understands how I feel. Everyone keeps on staring at me and whispering to each other. What's wrong with them? Or better questions is what's wrong with me? Why are they whispering?

90

Dammit! My pants don't fit my waist anymore. I need a belt desperately. I need new pants. I was stuck wearing a faded, wrinkly hospital gown. Oh well… at least I know my weight loss plan was working. I was happy to see the numbers on the scale dropping. Actually, to be honest, I like being 90 lbs. I don't think I need to lose anymore weight.

I saw the doctor again today. He's becoming more concerned with my weight. He wouldn't let me out on any passes until I gained some weight. WHAT? That's bullshit! I'm still walking around this shit-hole fine. I have enough energy to go out and do stuff. What the hell are you talking about? This is a flippin' psych ward! It has nothing to do with my weight! He can't hold that against me! That's so unfair!

I was in tears by the time I was finished with the doctor. I just flopped on my bed and cried until I couldn't anymore. I was all out of breath. My eyes stung from crying so much. I hate this. I hate my life! I thought I showed him long enough that I wasn't having any suicidal actions anymore. I've been here for 2 months. And now, I get denied a pass because of my weight. I'm also being put on freaking anti-psychotic meds to make me gain weight. Seroquil, then Olanzapine. None of them did me any good except keeping me bed-ridden for the week since I got so dizzy from them. I completely lost my equilibrium. Sure, asshole! Make me gain 10 flippin' pounds after my hard work to lose them. I hate you! I want OFF the stupid medicines. I'm getting headaches from them, and I can't even walk in a straight line. I'm not flippin' psychotic. I don't see things! I don't hear things!

100

The psychiatrist took me off the medications because of my evident complaints. He was happy that I have gained a satisfying amount of weight within a week. He said I could go on a pass. Yes! After being in here for 2 ½ months, I can finally go out and breathe non-hospital air!

I ran into my room and put my summer clothes on and dashed out the door like a little kid. I enjoyed my time in the sun. Too bad it was such a short pass. I had to go back in 4 hours. That sucks. But I can't complain. At least I can slowly regain my freedom. I guess the saying "All good things come to an end" is true.
I'm looking forward to my next pass, which will be longer.

I continue to progress well in the hospital. I didn't attempt suicide again. I felt good to be out. I want to be discharged. But what the hell. The doctor made the referral to Surrey Memorial Hospital's Adolescent Psych. Unit for me to be an inpatient and hopefully be in a more positive and supportive environment. Another in-patient program. What good is this going to do? My intake date is next Wednesday!

Why am I glad and sad at the same time? I feel sad to leave this place. I've gotten to know the staff and people here so well.

I'll miss him. He was such a nice guy. I don't want to move to another hospital, but it doesn't look like there's a choice. I'm too young to be in this hospital.

97

Ok. I'm at Surrey Memorial now. Yeah, I guess I agree with the better environment. It's a smaller unit, but at least I get my own room and bathroom. Things are more structured. There are daily programs that run. I get to do group therapy with other people more my age. Every Wednesday, there's an outing. We sit together every Monday and have a meeting to decide what we want to do for meal prep and what our outing would be.

At first, I was really with the program and participated in almost everything. I felt happy for the first time in a long time. I almost forgot what it's like to be happy. It feels so good. *Be glad. Happiness is one of God's unlimited blessings! (psalm 34-2).*

It's almost October now. The kids here all have school day program. Since I've already graduated and moving towards nursing school, I could do my studying in my room. I'm taking a Medical First Responder course next course. I got some studying to do. To my surprise, the course was easier than I thought. I passed with flying colors! But of course, I couldn't meet the weight lifting component. 180 pounds with a partner! What a joke! Whatever, I can always ask for help. It doesn't matter.

It's July now. Oh my gosh, my grade 12 provincials are next month. I haven't even flipped open my biology textbook. I'm so going to fail. I have another English provincial. But I don't think English will be a problem for me. There is no way to study for an English exam. But biology is a different story. I was in school for the first term until I got hospitalized. I don't even know anything past that term. That's why I didn't graduate along with my class in June. I wasn't ready to write my provincials.

I'm so stressed out. I'm feeling overwhelmed. I'm so tired of flipping through pages and pages of notes. Nothing is sticking to my head. *O Lord, I am poured out like water, and all my bones are out of joint: my heart is like wax; it is melted in the midst of my bowels. I may tell all my bones. (psalm 22.14).* I'm getting so depressed again. I can't do anything right. I'm losing weight because of the stress. *Lord, make me to know mine end, and the measure of my days, what it is; that I may know how frail I am. (psalm 39.4) I direct my prayers to thee every morning. I came here to pray. For strength. For help. Guide me, O Lord!*
Sometimes, it helps to redirect attention to the Lord. He will hear us. He foresees everything. I trust and hope that He will help us. We are all weak without his guidance and help.

88

The shocking numbers on the scale tells me and the nursing staff how stressed I've been. I can't remember the last time I weighed less than 90 lbs. Maybe when I was in grade 4? I don't know.

My exams are done now that it's the end of August. I also got the results back. I did fairly well given my circumstances. I passed both and managed to pull a B in both courses for my final mark!

But why am I so depressed? I'm having self harm plans and urges again. I didn't tell anyone about them. I can't control them from coming. I wish I can.

My psychiatrist let me out on a pass today. I didn't tell her I was feeling suicidal and that I had a plan to kill myself. I was dishonest with her. What ended up happening was: I took 50 extra strength Tylenols and 20 sleeping pills and ended up in CCU in Burnaby Hospital because I overdosed at a friend's place in Burnaby. I totally regret it. I almost died. This wasn't my second time attempting suicide. Many of the other previous ones were not mentioned because it was too much to think about.

Couple days later, after I was medically stable, I was transferred back to APU in Surrey Hospital. I won't be getting any passes anytime soon. The psychiatrist talked to me and asked me why I did this. I couldn't come with an answer. I guess it all had to with my losing of control. I feel like I'm back in square one.

It was after this experience, I started actively restricting my food intake and let my weight drop to as low as it can get.

I was discharged mid-October to a group home since I can't keep myself safe with family. The government now has custody over me. I got a social worker assigned, who's my guardian. I stayed at Orenda House, a house for youths.

75

This is the lowest weight I've ever gone down to. I always felt so weak and had absolutely no energy to do anything. I was bed seeking most of the time. By this time, I had a therapist who talked much about eating disorders nowadays. My family doctor had flat out told me that I was really sick and that I was anorexic.

After hearing that, I was still in denial. I knew I had a problem. I just didn't want to admit it. I didn't want to change. I wanted to slowly kill myself. I didn't find life to be worth living.

I got into the Eating Disorders program at St. Paul's Hospital rather quickly because of my serious condition. Nonetheless, I still had to wait for 3 months.

I was getting more obsessive with my restrictions of food. I would sometimes skip meals and not eat and drink for 3 days. Then I would end up in emergency room for dehydration. The hospital gave me about 3 Liters of NaCl 0.9% and D5W to keep my fluids and sugars balanced. My electrolytes were so low and messed up.

This was a cry for help. I just didn't want to change. I'm not ready. I want the world to stop doing everything for me and just let me be.

My desire of control has taken over my mind. This time, it has gone way too far. But I can't just stop it. I don't know how to stop! I am so frustrated!

Every time I think of food. I want to throw up. I purposely starve myself until I pass out. Why am I doing this to myself? I don't want any attention. But yet, when I get the attention, I get mad. When I don't get attention, I also get mad. Why is this so complicated and contradicting? What's going on with my mind? It's playing tricks on me. I can't wait anymore. I can't do this anymore.

85

Here we go. Psychosocial. Research. Physical Exam. The three "mandatory" components of the Eating Disorders Assessment. Anxious and depressed, I walked into the elevator of the hospital. Level 4. The small, old cube moved up slowly, floor by floor. Ding and out. I walked into the assessment office, where the team met me for the first time. Questions? Answers. Hesitation. Break. Into the exam room of an internist, an expert and guru of eating disorders: let the truth unravel. After thorough exam of my whole body, a diagnosis was made: Anorexia Nervosa, restrictive subtype. The sinister ring of "Anorexia" echoed in my head. That was when the bomb dropped. Silence. Treatment recommendations: tube feeding, magnesium IV infusions and other IV fluids. This is just the medically stabilization part. What about the therapy part? More counseling? More therapy? I already have a therapist. Do I have to go through more coping skills groups? Am I ready to give up the insensible control and obsession over food? Did they say hospitalization? My own little world was interrupted. How dare you? What's the deal? What's happening to me? You can't control me, for I have my own silent mastermind... Control. Food is disgusting. Fear. What's next?

As I'm getting ready for a medical priority bed, 3rd on the waitlist, my weight became a little more stable. I gained a little bit of weight while waiting to be assessed.

I guess now I'm just waiting for a bed. I'll go in as a voluntary patient, but if I threaten to leave the unit, a doctor will certify me under the mental health act and make me stay there until I'm medically and psychiatrically stable. I'm scared. I'm so anxious of this. This is going to be a life changing experience. I'm going to get a tube stuck up my nose and into my stomach for initiation of re-nourishment until I can try to eat more normally and gain some weight.

I didn't even realize I was this sick until after my assessment. Never have I thought about getting hospitalized again. Let alone getting tube-fed and a lot of IV's for hydration. They're going to draw blood from me almost every single day. Basically, I'll be in an ICU specially designed for people with eating disorders. I'm not anticipating this. I'm so scared. *I will say unto God my rock, Why hast thou forgotten me? Why go I in mourning because of the oppression of the enemy? As with a sword in my bones, mine enemies reproach me; while they say daily unto me, Where is why God? (psalm 42.9)*

I've been so absorbed into the evil world of control being the main focus. I've forgotten all about God. I've been so unfaithful. God gave me life. I can't believe myself. I'm trying to kill myself. Why am I still praying? Why do I doubt God now? Is he going to help me get better? O, Lord, please forgive my unfaithfulness.

Part Two:
Pre-hospitalization

86

There's a price for everything. Life's suffering is a small price to pay to get to our paradise. I'm getting weaker, requiring more bed rest at home. I spend most of my days in my bedroom. Onsets of fainting spells are rather frequent nowadays. Of course, I do have times when I'm up; usually I'm writing, reading, on my laptop chatting or surfing the net. I enjoy spending time with my friends too, but there's never enough time. We're all too busy.

I'm holding on with all the strength I have left. Lord, please hold me tight and give me thy strength.

I'm torn between choosing life or death. What keeps me from wanting to live? Sometimes, I just don't see the point of living. I can't think of anything to live for. Though, I can think up a million things to die for. Why is it that I'm always so pessimistic? Or is it just reality?

I had a dream. I was on top of a waterslide, slowly slipping downwards into the unknown deepness of water. Though, I know how to swim, but it was a weird feeling of not knowing. I held on tight to the sides. I was torn between whether I should let go or hold on. I think this is a message of some kind. I didn't let go in the dream. I held on. The repeated words I heard in my dream *"I don't wanna let go! Do I? Oh my god! I'm sliding. I'm going to let go."* were creepy. It was like a reality dream. It was kind of freaky.

◆   ◆   ◆

I don't know what and how I should feel. I got my admission date to the Extra Care Unit at the Eating Disorders Program. I felt grateful for a while. It wasn't that far away. Only 2 weeks. But I feel stressed out as well. I'm right in the middle of moving out on my own to another Elizabeth Fry Society's housing, only more independent. Also, I'm just absorbing the hospitalization news and I feel scared and anxious. I'm dealing with the RCMP as well, for what happened in the past. My parents found out everything, my brother told them when my social worker asked if anyone witnessed the abuse by my cousin. I feel guilty and I just feel that everything is my fault. I don't want to talk about it with anyone. I feel so weak. I don't want other young victims in the future, but I also don't want to see a family fight and seeing my cousin's future altered in any bad way. But I need to report this. What if it does happen again in the future to another innocent soul? How will I cope if I don't let this out? Who needs to be responsible for the actions? My therapist talked with me and helped me process my thoughts. I feel so mixed up. Nevertheless, I'm going to continue with pressing charges. I think this is the only reasonable way to make him responsible for his actions, to let it out of my soul to deal and cope with what happened, and to make certain of safety for myself and others.

So much for self blame. I've been told so many times this isn't my fault and that I don't have to be guilty, but yet I do feel all those feelings. I didn't go to my brother and younger cousin's graduation ceremony. Because I knew my cousin who sexually abused me was going to be there watching his brother walk across the stage. I told my mom not to pick me up from my apartment and that I felt sick. It was a lie. I feel bad not being able to watch my own brother walk across the stage. I hope I didn't hurt his feelings. I feel like a useless person who doesn't know how to deal or cope with anything. This is becoming too much. I can't take the stressors anymore. I never got to graduate with my class because of my hospitalization, but it was not an intention to make my brother feel bad or hurt him. It's me who can't face my troubling thoughts. It is I who can't put down the thoughts.

As my mind is unclear, I am restless, comatose, running on little or no sleep at all despite all the sleeping medication I take. My admission date has been pushed back to June 12, because the bed is not yet available. Another 2 weeks to wait. I don't know. I felt more relieved when I heard about the later admission date. Is that a good or bad thing?

82

I lost 2 lbs. in 2 days. I'm stressed. I haven't been eating as usual. Not enough fluids either. I fainted at a friend's house, and ended up going to Surrey Memorial Hospital, waiting overnight just to see a flippin' doctor. I hate that hospital. They have no idea what they're doing. They don't even know how to treat me. For the whole time, I was nauseous, dizzy, and having a headache. As well, I was having tachycardia. I knew I was dehydrated. I feel like that every time when I need IV fluids. Although, after long hours of waiting to see a doctor, he just gave me a Gravol injection and said drink lots of water, then discharged me. Oh… ok. So I went home and slept. I woke up nauseous and not wanting to eat or drink. I don't want to go to anymore hospitals, although Royal Columbian Hospital is right out my door.

◆   ◆   ◆

Just 4 more days before my admission to St. Paul's Hospital. I am so scared, anxious, angry… all emotions seem to mix together. I don't want to give up my control. Not yet.

I locked myself in my apartment for 2 days. Shut the blinds and just felt super cold. Before the 2 days… I was all too busy getting IV drips at the hospital for 7 hours straight: 2L 0.9% NaCl, 25mg Gravol, some multivitamins, 2mg MgSO4 with NS (NaCl), 1L KCl with NS and D5W (2 hours by infusion pump). The hospital checked my blood work. Pretty much everything was out of whack, especially my electrolytes. On top of that, they found a UTI and put me on antibiotics for 3 days… which didn't help much at all since I still have symptoms of an UTI, and my left side of my abdomen hurts so bad. I'm worried if it's a kidney infection or not.

What was really hard to believe was the fact that I turned so anemic in a week's time. My Hgb counts were at 124g/L, 120 being normal. And somehow it dropped to 103. I can't believe I didn't catch that. How could I not have noticed? No wonder I've been so tired and sleeping so much lately. No wonder I've been shivering and feeling cold on warm, sunny days. I had the heater up to full blast for the 2 days I locked myself in. I had something to eat. I took my normal meds as usual. I'm not sure why my blood levels would drop all so suddenly. I haven't been getting my period. I don't know where the blood's going.

◆   ◆   ◆

1 more day. I tried to cut off all my connections and detach with my friends yesterday. I pissed them off and said hurtful words to them, because I don't want them to see me go through this. I don't need to traumatize them by watching tubes going into me everywhere.

Part Three:
Hospitalization Journal

84

Day 1 of hospitalization. June 12, 2007. Meeting with a part of the care team didn't go so bad. Everyone's pretty nice here. Putting in the feeding tube in wasn't so bad. It didn't hurt as much as I had experienced with the charcoal tube put into me from overdoses. This one is a lot smaller and more flexible. I'm still getting used to it. My hemoglobin count was 107. It went a little bit up from June 7th.

Day 2 was a little easier to keep myself occupied. I watched a DVD I brought with me. I only have so many. I have to save them for later. Now that I have my laptop, I can write and journal here. I'm still trying to get used to the environment and the tubes and everything. I had blood work earlier today again. My hemoglobin count dropped to 97. Uh-oh. My care team can't figure out why I'm anemic either. They're going to talk with my hematologist about it. They checked my iron and my vitamin B12 levels, those were fine. I guess it'll take some time to find out what kind of anemia I have. I was actually quite hungry today and finished all my meals. I think I'm going to live. I'll be ok. I'm hoping to get out in 3 weeks, as planned originally. My preoccupation with food was just too much. But God heard my cry. I'm happy he's listening and guiding me.

Hear my prayer, O God, give ear to the words of my mouth. (Psalms 54:2)

He was always there, by my side, no matter what. He never left me and will never leave me. I have faith in Him. *O, I love You, dear Lord! I cannot ever thank you enough! I will keep saying my prayers to You. I know You are here with me no matter what.*

I was started on MgSO4 IV infusion today. I was also given a lot of oral pills to take to help my tube feed go smoother: potassium, sodium phosphate, thiamine, B12, and lots of other things to get me through. I'm looking forward to leaving here. I'm waiting for that day to come:

Our Father, who art in heaven,
hallowed be thy name.
Thy Kingdom come,
thy will be done,
on earth as it is in heaven
Give us this day our daily bread.
And forgive us our trespasses,
as we forgive those who trespass against us.
And lead us not into temptation,
but deliver us from evil.
For thine is the kingdom, the power and the glory. For ever and ever. Amen.

Day 3 of being in the ward. It seems less stressful. I'm beginning to get used to things and time schedules. I know when I have to take my meds, I know when I get my MgSo4 infusions. I'm kept on NS (normal saline) 100mL/ hour maintenance therapy. The doctors think I need it.

As usual, this is the third doctor I've met today. She, too was concerned about my anemia and was mentioning something about blood transfusions being the last resort. But the talk of this is becoming more and more focal. It was reinforced to me that I am very, very critically ill. I didn't think I was that bad. I still don't think I'm that bad. I keep thinking that there are always people worst off than me. It may be true. But that's not what I'm seeing in the ward. I'm the only one on bed rest. I'm the youngest one. I'm the also the only one of both IV's and tube feed. I also don't join groups nor do I get to socialize with other people. Maybe I will get to do some of those things when I'm considered less critically ill. I wonder when I can be off bed rest. But it seems pretty important to everyone that I'm on bed rest. Everyone is quite concerned about me. I am the skinniest girl on the ward, also the weakest.

I didn't have such a great day today. I had night sweats again. I woke up at 7am freezing cold and wanted a warm bath. Someone was in the bath… so I had to wait till after breakfast to have one. But I did get a chance to have a nice, long and warm bath. I felt way better after. But not to my surprise, I felt lightheaded and so dizzy I had to sit down. I felt very faint. I got out of the bath. Got dressed. Went to my room and dried my hair. I was sitting down for a while. I was still pretty dizzy. Anemia? Most likely, says the doctor. She wanted to run more tests to see if my body is producing RBC's, then consider the blood transfusion. I don't know. I feel pretty weak and crappy. I think I prefer the transfusion, even if there are risks. I want to feel stronger and be able to take a short walk without having chest pains and getting short of breath and dizzy. I don't want the fainting spells anymore. But I guess we'll have to see what the blood work shows tomorrow. Also, the doctor ordered a glucagons test on my liver to see if my insulin and glucagons levels are balancing and working properly.

Crap. I think I might have caught the cold. I can't stop sniffling. My nose is running all the time. This sucks. Kidney infection. Anemia. Cold. Not fun at all. I hope my kidney infection would be cleared up soon. And I don't want a cold now either. Go away. Leave me alone.

Day 4. Got poked so many times today. It wasn't even funny. It hurt. My arms are all bruised up. My IV decides to go interstitial now as well... so I get another IV restarted. I'm not having a blood transfusion... but they still couldn't find out why I'm anemic. I still feel dizzy. I feel nauseated from so much of the tube feed. My NG Tube is starting to irritate my nose. My nose is runny all the flippin' time now. I'm sniffling a lot. Man. I hate this! I hate being on bed rest. I can't do anything! Get me out of this shit hole!

Great! I got my results back from my glucagons test. I didn't pass. I have to stay on the tube feed. The doctor was in a rush to get to rounds... so she said she'll come back and talk to me later. My liver is unable to stabilize my blood sugar... and that's bad. I'm screwed. Flat line. I just felt like puking after I got that stupid glucagons injection. I didn't feel sugar level highs... I guess my liver is pretty screwed after all the damages have been done. They'll rerun the test next Wednesday to see if my liver is any better. Shit! I wanna get the hell outta here. All the poking and prodding didn't get me anywhere. I didn't pass the test. I feel like crap. I've been playing pinball to let my anger out. I've been banging on my keyboard and I guess venting on here! I think I'm going to break my laptop soon! I am so mad! And the IV Team still hasn't come up to restart my flippin' IV yet. Meaning I get to have another poke. I guess it's a good thing for now. I'm seriously not looking forward to lend them my arm for yet another experiment! Getting poked so many times... then they couldn't find any veins last time and had to use my other arm. My other is sore now... so they can't use it either. They better get this IV started in one go this time. Or I am going to flip! I so want to scream and cry! I just wanna act like a baby: kick and scream... not caring about what others say or hear. Oh great… as I just said about the IV… they're restarting it now!! Goddammit!!!

Alright. It wasn't that bad. She got it in with one try. My veins collapse every 2 days. Great! I hate it. More poking and prodding. I asked to keep the syringe. The lady gave it to me… but the nurses took it away… and all the other ones I've been collecting! Argh~! I hate you all!

At least I've got visitors coming to see me today… I guess something to look forward to IF they show up and not disappoint me. I've been disappointed too many times today. I don't need any more disappointments. I just want to cry! Ahh!

Day 5 feels pretty calm. For now anyway. I read three books, gave myself a French manicure. I was pleased with the results. All the nurses told me my nails were beautiful. I think so too. I was quite disappointed yesterday. None of my friends showed up to visit me as they promised. How I hate this! Or how I hate them? They don't understand what it's like to be on bed rest, bedridden. I lie around in my bed all day, including meal times, I sit in my bed and eat. I look out my window. Sometimes I see beautiful sunshine, sometimes the dark clouds depresses me. But how I wish to be outside, just for a breath of fresh air. People don't understand that all I do is bedridden activities and anticipate visitors. Just to have someone to talk to. To connect with the outside world. I hate how they all say they'll be coming or they'd be here and not show up. They don't even bother calling me to tell me they're not coming. I waited and waited, from dawn to dusk, wondering what went wrong. Did they not want to see me? Why don't they just tell me they don't want to come see me? I would understand. Hospitals aren't for everyone, especially not in this ward. I was pretty depressed about yesterday.

I distracted myself with books, journaling, and gave myself a manicure. I slept well. I think it was because I didn't get much sleep ever since I've been admitted with all those tests the doctors had to run. I was all worked up yesterday. I fell asleep after taking my sleeping pills.

I ate all my breakfast. Pancakes. One of my favorite breakfast foods. I didn't finish my lunch. This was the first time. To replace what I didn't finish, the nurses had to shoot some more Resource Plus into the side port of my tube feed, which was already Resource Plus. Every time I don't finish my food, the nurses get a big syringe and shoot more nutrients up into my tube feed.

I'm having my MgSO4 infusion now. It's running rather slow because of my delicate veins and constant collapsing of them. It's running at 75mL/hour. It normally takes 4 hours to infuse the 500mL bag, but this will take longer than 4 hours, since the flow rate is slower to reduce the irritability. It's 14:29. I wonder if I'll get any visitors. Surprise me. Wake me. I'm so exhausted now. I need to nap.

18:34. MgSO4 infusion still going, almost done though. VTBI = 2.6mL… yea! I didn't finish my dinner, so they had to put some Resource Plus by syringe into my tube feed again. Why am I not surprised.

I'm not even going to bother anticipating any visitors. I don't even care anymore. Let me be. Just leave me. Wasted. Why spend my entire life anticipating bullshit? Why believe people? Who EVER does what was said? Forget it. This is the reality of life. People are too preoccupied to care; too busy to make merely a phone call to say whether I should expect them or not. Or, even worse, people just forget about me. I'm cool with that when they are not true friends. Do they care?

Day 6 of treatment: here goes… my tube feed was blocked, so the nurses had to pull it out and get a doctor to restart another one. It was kind of painful and uncomfortable… but after awhile, you get used to it. I'm still having the cold. My last day of MgSO4 infusion is today, started officially at 16:35. From now on, they have to collect my urine for 24 hours to see how much of the Magnesium my body retained.

To make matters worse, of course, my IV site just had to collapse today too. I had to be poked twice before the IV nurse got a line in my arm successfully.

I went on a little wheelchair trip with the porter today to the radiology department for an x-ray of where and how well my NG tube was sitting this time. It was a fast trip, but at least I got to get out of the ward for a little bit. I wouldn't say it was a bad thing, even though the trip drained my energy. I had to gather up energy to stand for 10 minutes when the x-ray technician set everything up and have me x-rayed. I was quite dizzy after. I see the doctor's point now: why am I on bed rest?

My birthday is fast approaching. Friday. June 22. That's in 5 days. I will likely spend yet another birthday in the hospital. Except I'll be turning 19 this year and I won't be receiving a long pass or if I even get one. Because

I'm medically unstable and on the tube feed, it makes passes very challenging since I have to be closely monitored 24/7.

It's dinner time in about 15 minutes. I was going to take a nap… but there's not much of a point now, is there? Maybe after dinner, I'll nap a little bit. My friend's supposed to come see me today, but I dare not anticipate anything or anyone. I am so sick and tired of broken, unkept promises. Life is just so full of those. Boring. Old news.

Sometimes, I seriously wish I was dead. I'm not suicidal, but I just really don't see the point of fighting so hard for life sometimes. But I guess that's up to God. *He won't give us anything harder than we can handle. As long as we trust Him, He'll guide us through. Pray, and He listens. He will take our hand and walk us through every step of our life. We are never alone. Therefore, I'm not afraid of death. I think life is just something we have to get through to get to our paradise, Heaven!*

I love this passage. It's my all time favorite. It sounds depressing, but I believe it's true. I would love for this verse to be read out at my own funeral (not that I'm going to kill myself), but here it is:
"The Lord is my shepherd; I shall not want. He maketh me to lie down in green pastures: he leadeth me beside the still waters. He restoreth my soul: he leadeth me in the paths of righteousness for his name's sake. Yea, though I walk through the valley of the shadow of death, I will fear no evil: for thou art with me; thy rod and thy staff they comfort me. Thou preparest a table before me in the presence of mine enemies: thou anointest my head with oil; my cup runneth over. Surely goodness and mercy shall follow me all the days of my life: and I will dwell in the house of the Lord for ever." (psalms 23:1)

It's Father's Day today. I didn't call my family, yet. Or will I ever? I don't want to talk to them. I don't want to be bombarded by questions. Most certainly, I don't want to see them. It's just one of those days. Lazy and irresponsible. I've been here for almost a week now, and haven't bothered to call RCMP to update them with a phone number that they can actually contact me by. Of course, I don't know the case progress either if I haven't kept in touch with them. I guess it's an avoidance thing. I've been trying to avoid a lot of things ever since I've been here. I've been avoiding friends, family, and just people in general. When I'm outside of here, I have to deal with things head on. There're no chances for hiding and avoiding things. I want out of here ASAP. I have a feeling that my eating and everything done here to help me will all be reversed to my old habits again when I get discharged here. It's like

I don't feel like changing. I'm not ready. But I'm also not stubborn, because if I was, I wouldn't voluntarily be here in the first place. Of course, after I get admitted, it's not really about the voluntary part anymore. It's all based on how medically stable I am. I hope I'll be so soon enough, so I can leave. But if I do end up so thin again, if not worse, what are the chances of me coming back here? None. Nada. Zilch. Zero. I will not voluntarily admit myself to any hospital. I hate this. Being in my bed all the time, anything more exciting to do? No I don't want to join the flippin' retarded groups. I want out. I want my own bed, my own space, and most of all, my apartment. I am so homesick. Of course, there's no hope or chance for recovery in this short period of time. Will I ever get better? Perhaps not. What therapy? I've had nothing so far. I've seen psychiatry, but she's kind of useless. I just feel way better when I'm not stuck in the hospital.

Day 7 as of today. I haven't been feeling well for the past 2 days. I haven't been finishing my food. They have had to push 300mL/hour into my tube feed. I feel like crap. I feel like throwing up every time they do it. As of now, they're doing it. They've done it for 2 meals today. I just can't eat. I'm so sick and tired of food. My stomach hurts. I can't tolerate any food anymore. And I have my glucagons liver test tomorrow, so I won't be getting much sleep tonight. I'll be poked and prodded for many times. I just have to pass it this time. I really want to be discharged. I need to be out of here. I want to cry. I just can't stand staying in bed anymore. I miss my home. I hate it here! I hate myself! I get weighed tomorrow as well. I don't want to know! I don't want to know how much weight I gained! I feel so fat now. I can't even bear looking myself in the mirror anymore. I need to stop thinking now! I need to stop it!

I just don't know what else is going on anymore. My boobs hurt so much. It feels like they're getting heavier. It could be the pill. I've never had big boobs to start with… but then again, can my weight gain lead to some of this? But I've been heavier before, and it didn't hurt or felt this weird before. My bra hardly fits me anymore. I am hopeless.

I really want to go home. I'm really tired of everything.

88

Day 8. How time flies. I got weighed today. I gained 4lbs. in 8 days. Holy crap! And I also got a repeat glucagons liver function test. I failed it again. I'll get a repeat test on Monday, because I told the care team I really want to be out of here. I'm so sick and tired of staying on bed rest. I hate it! My IV collapsed again. Even if I don't have to have fluids through my IV, they said since I failed my liver test, they have to keep access to my veins in case my feeding tube blocks. They have to put in D5W as soon as possible in that case. I hope it doesn't happen. It was painful enough the first time.

My tube feed has increased from 45 to 85mL/hour now. They want to make sure I pass the test on Monday. I want to pass it, so I can go home. I miss home. But even if I pass it, it only means that they can take the feeding tube out… but as soon as my tube is out, they have to watch me and put me on IV's since I'm not getting quite as much nutrients. I guess that's still a step closer to discharge.

Day 9 means 1 day before my birthday. Looking outside through my window only depresses me more. The sun-kissed air and warmness that I can't feel; a fresh breath I can't take outside; another birthday spent in the hospital. 19. Will I grow up and learn something?

I still feel so fat. When I look in the mirror, I see a fat girl. I don't believe in miracles. I don't think this hospitalization is going to change anything for me.

At least I can start going to leisure groups now. I learnt how to make paper roses with tissue paper. They look quite real. I'm surprised at my artistic skills. I made lots to give away to my visitors. I also had a paraffin wax manicure treatment here. It felt nice to put your hands in warm wax and then peel it off and make shapes out of the soft wax until it hardens. Other than these leisure groups I enjoy, there's not much pleasurable here, especially when I have to be in my bed 24/7. If all goes well, I'm expecting my family counselor to visit soon with her dog, Olive. Too bad she can't bring Mocha, the dog that I love so much at the group home. I'm sure she's grown a wee bit bigger. I miss her so much. I can only look at pictures on my laptop. I want to hold her and feel her with my hands. I miss her kisses. I miss the outside world. Not that I don't miss Olive, but Mocha and I bonded when she was so young. There's something special between us. I know she loves me. I'm just imagining next time I get to see her, she'll just be so happy and be jumping up and down, hopping on my leg waiting for me to pick her up and cuddle with her. I miss playing with her. I love you, Mocha. Thinking of Mocha motivates me and makes me want to get out of here sooner. I can't wait.

17:40 – I didn't finish my dinner. I feel sick to my stomach. I feel dizzy and nauseous. I'm twitching a lot too. My muscles are doing funny things. How annoying.

Day 10. June 22, 2007. Happy birthday to me. 19. What a number. I'm officially an adult now. I'm not too excited… probably because I'm stuck in bed.

I'm going to be getting more magnesium infusions because of the muscle cramps. I don't mind them. They're not too bad. I got blood work done today too. That wasn't fun. The lab lady had to poke me twice just to get one vial of blood. My veins are all hiding because of the numerous times they've been poked. Bruises all over my arms, it just doesn't look pretty at all.

Great. To top things off even more, I have to pee in a cup again. They want to check for infections. Argh… one thing after another. Now, I have to do a ECG again.

Day 11. Boring day. I had no visitors. My NG tube got clogged and had to be taken out. I was stuck on D10W, 10% dextrose to keep my sugars in normal range… but I felt hypoglycemic. I was so tired and weak all day. Then of course, MgSO4 infusion didn't help since it just completely stopped the flow of dextrose. A doctor came up later and inserted a new tube, x-rayed; everything is back on track now.

I had a lot of birthday visits and gifts. Thank you ever so kindly!

Day 15. I'm in some emotional distress here. I was last night anyway. I'm still disappointed and upset. I failed my liver glucagons test again. My NG tube clogged up again. I was on D10W the whole night… needing to get up and pee during the night. Last day of MgSO4 infusion. I have to do the Mag. Load again. Pee in a bottle for 24 hours. God. Help me, please! I'm sick and tired of that stupid tube always clogging up and having to get a new one in. The doctors put it too far down the last two times, which is probably why it clogged up so fast. They went in at 65cm. Today, this one went in at 55cm. What a difference. I hope this stays in longer. Pulling the tube out hurts a lot. It burns! Now I'm on normal saline, bolus, running the bag thru. Since I feel so much better with the NS IV, the doctor has ordered some for me. She told me that she'll keep me on that for a while. The Mag. Load will determine my magnesium levels. Hopefully I won't need anymore infusions. I had lots of hopes. I was hoping to pass the glucagons test, hoping my tube wouldn't collapse again, hoping to get out of here soon. I feel so stuck here. My muscles are cramping up for every single movement I do, even my stomach cramps up. Doc said something about maybe it's the bed rest and the lack of activity? She said it probably has nothing to do with my magnesium levels. She thinks I've received enough magnesium. That's at least one positive thing.

I just finished talking to the dietitian, she's bumping my tube feed up to 100mL/hr. Well… I can say I'm not too happy, but I do want to get out of here. She did make a very good point. So I guess all I can do is follow it.

Emotionally, I'm still feeling pretty down. I don't know what is going to fight this feeling away. Definitely bed rest isn't going to help it. I just want to cry and call it quits. I don't want to do this anymore. I want to scream and throw my meal tray on the ground, have a fit, yell some more, and stomp out of the ward with all my stuff. I want to leave. I just wish that this was it! I want to say it's OVER! THE END. But realistically, I can't do that, because I know I'm going to get certified and that puts me into more psychological disturbances. I'm going to hold it till the very end. Until I seriously can't stand it anymore, which I think am pretty close… meanwhile, calm myself down and use thought stopping techniques to stop myself from doing anything violent or stupid. Writing helps. That's why I'm doing it.

95

Day 18. Holy shit! I gained so much weight I think I must be at least 100 lbs by now. I look sooooo fat. OMG! This is so ugly! I can't believe this is happening!

I might get discharged on Wednesday if I pass my glucagons test on the same day. Let's hope I pass it. I can't stand being here anymore! Seriously, I'm going to go insane! I am so going to lose fucking 10 lbs. when I get out. I look way too fat now. There's no way in hell I'm going to maintain this weight or gain more. I look like a giant marshmallow with fat squishing out everywhere and IV marks all over my arms. I look like a druggy.

My NG tube clogged up this morning again. The doctor came by in the afternoon to put a new one in. It went smoothly. However, my IV site was not so smooth. It went interstitial and swelled my arm up like a balloon. My arm's all red too. The nurse had to take it out and put another one in. It sucked. Everything sucks.

◆　◆　◆

Ewww!!! This is nasty! I pulled the Leads from a heart monitor off my skin when I went to take a shower. My skin was all gooey and I found a rash with hives on my stomach. It hurts like hell! It looks like there was an allergic reaction to the gel that sticks to my skin. The hives and rash look like there were small welts growing on my skin. It looks so disgusting! There's some pus oozing out of it. I feel so gross. It hurts like hell when I tried to wash it with just water and soap. The soap stung like knives stabbing into my wound. This never happened before. I've worn those things so many times. Why does it decide to happen now? There's absolutely no way in hell am I reattaching new Leads onto my body and continue with the Holter Monitor for my heart! I can't stand this anymore! I need to get out of here! I need to get out next week or I'm going to go crazy as if I'm not already psychotic at times being trapped on a bed in a room staring at four walls long enough!

God, please save me! Please listen to my prayer. Hear my cry and watch my tears fall. I'm using all my strength I have to pray to You. Please help me out of here. I am in a lot of pain. I know You won't leave me in pain to suffer the unknown in the dark, right? You won't. I know You won't.

98

Day 22. I passed my glucagons test today. That means I get discharged. On Day 22! July 4, 2007. I can get out of here! I'm so excited! My last day!! I made it past 3 weeks! I can't wait until I get to breathe the outside air, see the outside world again.

It's weird standing outside. I'm not used to it. I feel so wobbly. I think it'll take some time to get used to.

I will be followed by outpatient eating disorders team following discharge. We'll see how I do after 3 months.

~ Epilogue ~

3 weeks after discharge...
I've lost 5 pounds. It's expected because I'm not on the tube feed 24/7. Will this hospital experience change my life forever? Will I be pronounced cured and rid of my anorexia? So many questions to be answered. But no answers can be given until they monitor me for about 6 months and see how my weight goes.

Watch for the next book. Title to be determined. Thank you, readers, for your support!

Printed in the United States
129733LV00001BC/16/P

9 780595 509751